ADELE

SINGING SENSATION

Big Buddy Books

An Imprint of Abdo Publishing
abdopublishing.com

BIG
BUDDY POP BIOGRAPHIES

KATIE LAJINESS

abdopublishing.com

Published by Abdo Publishing, a division of ABDO, PO Box 398166, Minneapolis, Minnesota 55439.
Copyright © 2018 by Abdo Consulting Group, Inc. International copyrights reserved in all countries.
No part of this book may be reproduced in any form without written permission from the publisher.
Big Buddy Books™ is a trademark and logo of Abdo Publishing.

Printed in the United States of America, North Mankato, Minnesota.
052017
092017

THIS BOOK CONTAINS RECYCLED MATERIALS

Cover Photo: Featureflash Photo Agency/Shutterstock.com.
Interior Photos: ASSOCIATED PRESS (pp. 6, 13, 15, 23, 25); Chris Pizzello/Invision/AP (pp. 17, 23);
    dpa picture alliance/Alamy Stock Photo (p. 19); Gilles Petard/Contributor/Getty (p. 9);
    John Shearer/Invision/AP (p. 17); Kevin Mazur/Contributor/Getty (p. 27); LaCameraChiara/
    Shutterstock.com (p. 11); Matt Sayles/Invision/AP (p. 29); PA Images/Alamy Stock Photo
    (p. 23); Pictorial Press Ltd/Alamy Stock Photo (p. 9); REUTERS/Alamy Stock Photo (p. 5); WENN
    Ltd/Alamy Stock Photo (pp. 11, 21).

Coordinating Series Editor: Tamara L. Britton
Graphic Design: Jenny Christensen

Publisher's Cataloging-in-Publication Data

Names: Lajiness, Katie, author.
Title: Adele / by Katie Lajiness.
Description: Minneapolis, MN : Abdo Publishing, 2018. | Series: Big buddy
    pop biographies | Includes bibliographical references and index.
Identifiers: LCCN 2016962357 | ISBN 9781532110573 (lib. bdg.) |
    ISBN 9781680788426 (ebook)
Subjects: LCSH: Adele, 1985- --Juvenile literature. | Singers--England--
    Biography--Juvenile literature.
Classification: DDC 782.42164092 [B]--dc23
LC record available at http://lccn.loc.gov/2016962357

CONTENTS

MUSIC SENSATION

Adele is a skilled **performer** and songwriter. With her strong voice, Adele's music is popular around the world. She has been **interviewed** for magazines and TV shows. And, Adele has won many **awards** for her hit albums and songs.

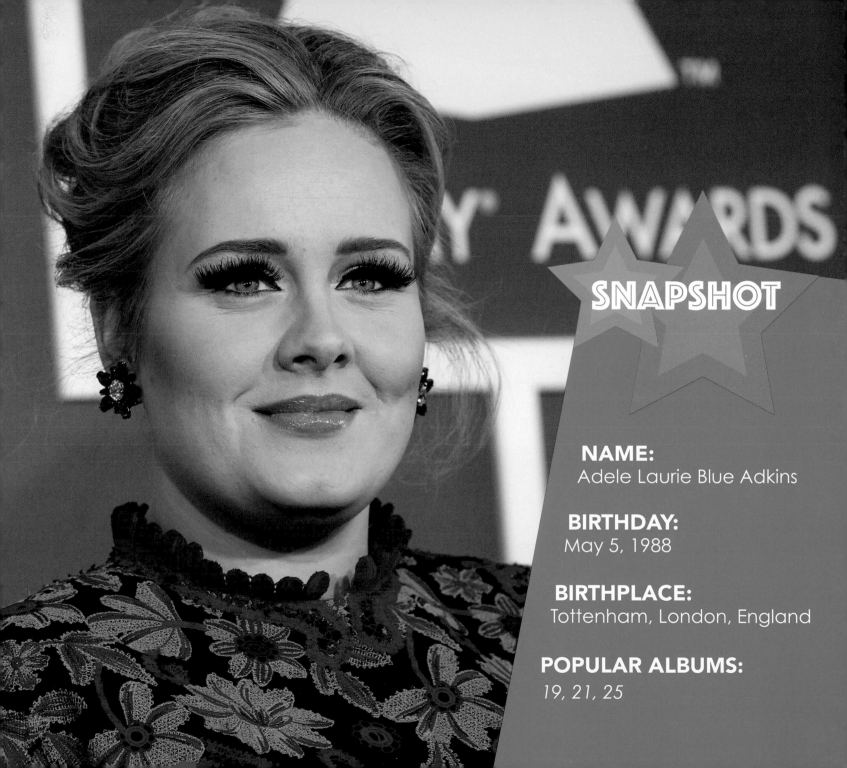

SNAPSHOT

NAME:
Adele Laurie Blue Adkins

BIRTHDAY:
May 5, 1988

BIRTHPLACE:
Tottenham, London, England

POPULAR ALBUMS:
19, 21, 25

FAMILY TIES

Adele Laurie Blue Adkins was born in Tottenham, London, England, on May 5, 1988. Her parents are Mark Evans and Penny Adkins. Adele has a younger half brother named Cameron.

Adele keeps her personal life private so pictures of her family are rare. But a lucky photographer caught Adele and her husband Simon at a concert in 2013.

WHERE IN THE WORLD?

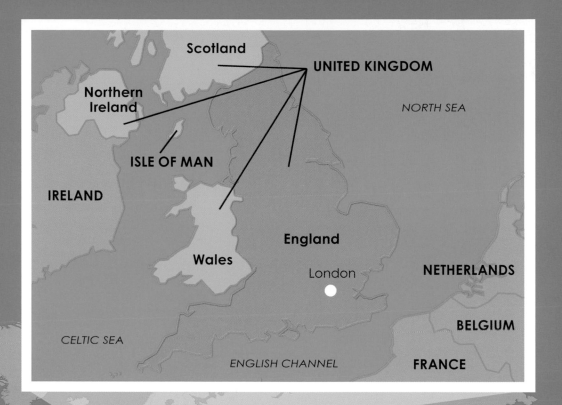

Scotland

UNITED KINGDOM

Northern
Ireland

NORTH SEA

ISLE OF MAN

IRELAND

England

Wales

London

NETHERLANDS

BELGIUM

CELTIC SEA

ENGLISH CHANNEL

FRANCE

EARLY YEARS

When Adele was three years old, her parents separated. So, Adele's mother worked hard to support her daughter. While Adele was growing up, the two moved often.

Adele began singing at a young age. As a teenager, she listened to famous singers such as Ella Fitzgerald and Etta James. She also enjoyed **pop** music.

In 1958, Ella Fitzgerald became the first African-American woman to win a Grammy Award. She went on to win 13 Grammys.

Etta James became a member of the Rock and Roll Hall of Fame in 1993.

RISING STAR

In 2002, Adele went to the BRIT School, a **performing** arts high school. While in school, Adele recorded three **demo** songs. One of her friends posted them on **social media**. Soon, a record company wanted to record Adele's music.

DID YOU KNOW ?
Adele's songs were very personal. Her fans felt like she was singing about their lives.

Adele attended the BRIT School with pop stars Leona Lewis *(left)* and Jessie J *(below)*.

11

GREAT SINGER

Adele's first album came out in 2008. It was called *19*. By the next year, it had sold 2.2 million copies in the United Kingdom.

In the United States, Adele sang on *Saturday Night Live*. After her **performance**, album sales soared there. Over time, *19* sold more than 3 million copies in the United States.

In 2007, Adele won the first Critics' Choice Award at the BRIT Awards.

In 2011, Adele released her second album, *21*. That year, "Someone Like You" was number one on the Billboard Hot 10 chart. And, "Rolling in the Deep" was number one for seven weeks.

The album topped the music charts in more than 30 countries. In the United Kingdom, *21* is the fourth best-selling album of all time. In the United States, it sold more than 11 million copies!

DID YOU KNOW ?
Adele's album titles are named for the age she was when she recorded them.

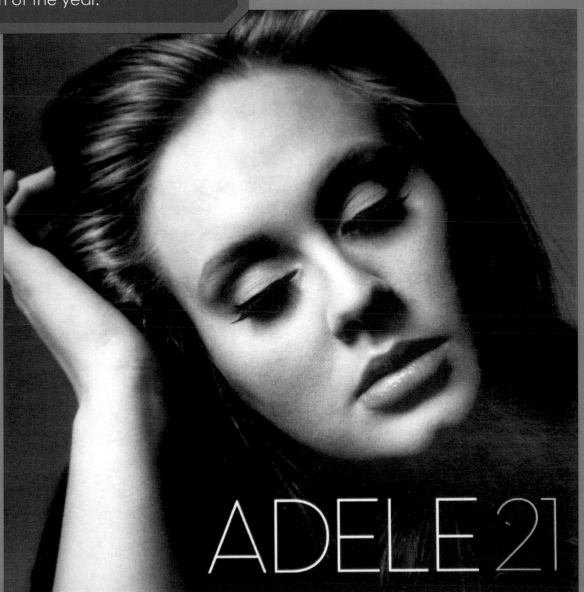

In 2015, Billboard announced Adele's *21* was the biggest-selling album of the year.

15

SUPERSTAR

After two hit albums, Adele was a singing star. In 2012, she wrote and sang "Skyfall" for a movie. At the **Grammy Awards**, Adele sang the song live for the first time.

The single went on to sell 1.3 million **digital** copies. Adele won both an **Academy Award** and a Grammy Award for the song.

In 2013, Adele sang "Skyfall" with a live orchestra at the Academy Awards.

Adele is one of few artists to win an Academy Award (*shown*), a Grammy Award, and a Golden Globe Award.

Adele's third album, *25*, came out in
2015. In its first week, it sold nearly 3.5 million
copies. It went on to sell more than 10 million
copies in the United States.

"Hello" became the album's top song.
It was one of the best-selling singles of
the year. In the United States, it was
downloaded 1.1 million times in one week.

During its first week, *25* sold 335 albums every minute!

ON TOUR

Adele has done three world tours. In February 2016, she took her latest show on the road. It kicked off in Belfast, Ireland.

For this tour, Adele **performed** in more than 100 shows. The last concert was in London, England, on July 2, 2017.

DID YOU KNOW?

Adele deals with stage fright. Singer Beyoncé helped Adele handle her fears to feel more confident on stage.

During her concerts, Adele often invites fans to join her on stage.

AWARDS AND HONORS

Over the years, Adele has won many **awards**. In 2009, she won **Grammy Awards** for Best New Artist and Best Female **Pop** Vocal **Performance**.

In 2012, Adele took home six Grammy Awards. Five years later, Adele won five more Grammys. Both times, she took home the Album of the Year and Song of the Year awards.

In 2013, Adele accepted the Most Excellent Order of the British Empire from Prince Charles.

In 2012 (*above*) and 2017 (*left*), Adele won every Grammy Award she was nominated for.

OFF THE STAGE

Offstage, Adele tries to lead a normal life. In 2011, she had **surgery** on her throat. Adele took time off to get better.

Family is important to Adele. She began dating Simon Konecki in 2011. Their son, Angelo James Konecki, was born on October 19, 2012. Adele and Simon married in 2017.

In 2015, Simon joined Adele at the Glastonbury Festival in England.

GIVING BACK

Adele enjoys giving back to **charities**. She has **performed** at many benefit concerts. Her singing has helped Keep a Child Alive, Pride London, and MusiCares.

She also works with Simon Konecki's nonprofit called Drop4Drop. This organization helps bring clean water to people around the world.

In 2008, Adele and singer Alicia Keys (*right*) attended a ball for Keep a Child Alive. This charity raises money to fight an illness called AIDS.

BUZZ

After Adele's world tour in 2017, she plans to take a break. During this time, Adele wants to spend more time with Simon and Angelo.

Adele is a gifted artist with a powerful voice. Her music tells personal stories people can relate to. Fans are excited to see what Adele does next!

Adele sang her hit song "Hello" at the 2017 Grammy Awards.

GLOSSARY

Academy Award an award given by the Academy of Motion Picture Arts and Sciences to the best actors and filmmakers of the year.

award something that is given in recognition of good work or a good act.

charity a group or a fund that helps people in need.

demo a recording to show a musical group or artist's abilities.

digital using computer technology.

Grammy Award any of the awards given each year by the National Academy of Recording Arts and Sciences. Grammy Awards honor the year's best accomplishments in music.

interview to ask someone a series of questions.

perform to do something in front of an audience. A performer is someone who performs. A performance is the act of doing something, such as singing or acting, in front of an audience.

pop relating to popular music.

social media a form of communication on the Internet where people can share information, messages, and videos. It may include blogs and online groups.

surgery (SUHRJ-ree) the treating of sickness or injury by cutting into and repairing body parts.

WEBSITES

To learn more about Pop Biographies, visit **abdobooklinks.com**. These links are routinely monitored and updated to provide the most current information available.

INDEX